Home Activities

Dorothy S. Strickland
Richard F. Abrahamson
Roger C. Farr
Nancy R. McGee
Nancy L. Roser

HBJ
LANGUAGE

4

Karen S. Kutiper
Patricia Smith

HARCOURT BRACE JOVANOVICH, PUBLISHERS

Orlando   San Diego   Chicago   Dallas

ISBN 0-15-316630-4

HOME ACTIVITIES

Contents

To the Teacher

The *Home Activities* suggest activities that students and family members can do together outside the classroom to practice and reinforce language arts skills presented in *HBJ Language*. There is one home activity copying master for each Reading with a Writer's Eye lesson, each Thinking as a Writer lesson, each Developing the Writer's Craft lesson, each Writing Process series of lessons, and each grammar lesson. Select appropriate home activities whenever you believe students would benefit from the additional practice and encouragement from family members. The home activity copying masters are available both in English and in Spanish.

5 | Writing a Personal Narrative

Write a personal narrative to share with your family. Ask a family member to help you.

1. On the lines, make a list of things you have done outdoors. Circle the topic you like best.

_____

_____

_____

_____

_____

_____

_____

_____

_____

_____

_____

_____

_____

2. Write a rough draft about your topic. Tell what you did in time order. Do not worry about spelling, punctuation, and grammar yet.

3. Read your narrative to a family member. Make changes to make the writing better.

4. Check your writing for errors in capitalization, punctuation, and grammar. Circle any words you think are misspelled. Find out how to spell them.

5. Make a clean copy of your narrative. Make sure there are no mistakes. Share your narrative with your family.

6 | Sentences

Complete this activity at home.

1. Write five sentences that tell about someone you saw on television or that you read about. Make sure that each sentence is a complete thought.

_____

_____

_____

_____

_____

_____

_____

_____

_____

_____

2. Read your sentences to a family member.

3. Ask your family member if he or she thinks your sentences give a good description of the person.

4. Use a suggestion from your family member to write two more sentences about the person you described.

_____

_____

_____

_____

_____

_____

_____

_____

_____

7 | Declarative and Interrogative Sentences

Plan a career interview of an older family member.

1. Decide which family member you want to interview. Then write five questions, or interrogative sentences, that you want to ask.

_____

_____

_____

_____

_____

_____

_____

_____

2. Read your questions to a partner. Cross out any questions that you both think are not good questions.

3. Use your questions to interview your family member. After the interview, write three declarative sentences that tell what you learned.

_____

_____

_____

_____

_____

_____

_____

_____

_____

8 Imperative and Exclamatory Sentences

Plan to teach a family member how to play your favorite game.

1. Think of a game you can play well.

2. Write four imperative sentences that tell how to play the game.

_____

_____

_____

_____

_____

_____

_____

_____

3. Write four exclamatory sentences that tell the person he or she is playing well.

_____

_____

_____

_____

_____

_____

_____

_____

_____

_____

9 | Subjects and Predicates

Complete this activity at home with a family member.

1. Think about a pet that you would like to own. Then write five sentences about your pet. Do not tell what the pet is.

_____

_____

_____

_____

_____

_____

_____

_____

2. Now mix up your sentences. Write the predicates with the wrong subjects. Try to make your mixed-up sentences funny.

_____

_____

_____

_____

_____

_____

_____

_____

3. Put a piece of paper over the first five sentences that you wrote.

4. Ask a family member to read your mixed-up sentences and tell you what your imaginary pet is.

10 Complete and Simple Subjects

Ask a family member to help you write a story about a storm.

1. Think about a storm that you remember. Maybe you have been outside in a rainstorm or a snowstorm.

2. Write a simple subject for the first sentence of your story.

_____

3. Ask a family member to tell you how to end the sentence. On the lines, write the simple subject and the ending of the sentence.

_____

_____

_____

4. If you need to, add words to make the sentence a complete thought.

5. Repeat steps 2, 3, and 4 until your story is complete. As you and your family member think of each new sentence, write the sentence on the lines.

_____

_____

_____

_____

_____

_____

_____

_____

_____

_____

_____

_____

11 Complete and Simple Predicates

Play this sentence game with a family member.

1. Ask a family member to play this game with you. Use five pieces of paper. Write a short sentence on each piece of paper. For example, you might write a sentence that reads, *Peggy jumped.*

2. Turn the papers over so that the sentences are hidden. Ask your family member to pick up one of the papers. Then ask him or her to add words that tell more about the sentence and that make the sentence funny. For example, the new sentence might read *Peggy jumped over the moon.*

3. Choose one of the pieces of paper yourself. Add words to the sentence on that piece of paper. Try to make your sentence funny.

4. When each sentence has had words added, read the sentences again.

5. Talk to the family memeber about the sentences. Decide which ones are the funniest. Write the two funniest sentences on the lines.

_____

_____

_____

_____

6. Draw two pictures to illustrate your funniest sentences.

12 Paragraph of Information

Complete this activity at home.

1. Find an information article in a magazine or newspaper. The topic should be something that interests you.

2. Read the article to yourself.

3. Ask a family member to read the same article.

4. Choose two paragraphs to discuss together.

5. Discuss the answers to the following questions.

   a. What did you learn that was new to you?

   _____

   _____

   _____

   _____

   b. Was there enough information in the paragraph? If not, what else should have been included?

   _____

   _____

   _____

   _____

   c. Could anything have been left out without changing the meaning? If so, what was it?

   _____

   _____

   _____

   _____

6. Take turns sharing the part of the article that you found most interesting. You may share by reading aloud or by telling about it in your own words.

13 Analyzing a Paragraph of Information

Make a game using topic sentences and detail sentences.

1. You will need 3″ x 5″ cards or paper cut into rectangles, a newspaper or magazine that you have permission to cut up, and paste or glue.

2. In the newspaper or magazine, find ten paragraphs that have good topic sentences. Cut them out.

3. Cut each topic sentence apart from the rest of the paragraph.

4. Paste or glue each topic sentence to a card. Paste or glue the rest of each paragraph to another card. You should have 20 cards. Ten will be topic-sentence cards. The other ten will be detail-sentence cards.

5. Ask a family member to play a game called Topics and Details with you, using your cards.

6. Mix all the cards, and lay them face down in a grid of four cards by five cards.

7. Players take turns. The first player turns over one card and reads it. Then the player turns over another card and reads it. If one card is a topic-sentence card and the other card is the detail-sentence card that goes with it, a match has been made. The player keeps the cards and takes another turn.

8. If the cards are not a match, both cards are turned face down in the original places and the other player takes a turn.

9. The person who has the most pairs of matching topic-sentence cards and detail-sentence cards at the end of the game is the winner.

14 Connecting Main Ideas and Details

Complete this activity at home.

1. Talk with an adult family member about a home appliance such as a microwave oven or a washing machine.

2. In the center of the box, write a main idea about the appliance you discussed. Circle the main idea. Write details around the main idea that tell about the appliance. Circle the details. Connect the main idea and the details with lines.

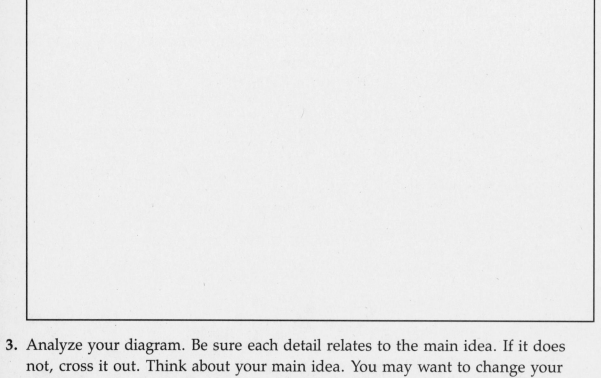

3. Analyze your diagram. Be sure each detail relates to the main idea. If it does not, cross it out. Think about your main idea. You may want to change your main idea sentence so that the detail sentences relate to it better. Redraw the diagram on another sheet of paper.

4. Show your diagram to the family member who talked to you about the topic. Ask him or her to help you decide whether you have included all the details related to the main idea.

15 Using Exact Words

Play this game at home with a family member.

1. Gather magazines from which you can cut out pictures.

2. Find pictures that fit into three broad categories. For example, you could look for pictures of dogs, pictures of people, and pictures of automobiles. Try to find at least five pictures for each category. Cut out each picture.

3. Mix up the pictures and spread them on a table.

4. Begin the game by giving a broad clue to your family member. For example, you might say, "I'm thinking of a picture of an automobile." The other person should try to guess which picture you have in mind.

5. If the correct picture isn't guessed on the first try, give a more exact clue. For example, you might say, "I'm thinking of a convertible."

6. Each time, give a more exact clue until the correct picture is guessed.

7. What kind of clues were least helpful to your family member?

_____

_____

_____

_____

_____

_____

8. What words in your clues made the clues most helpful to your family member?

_____

_____

_____

_____

_____

_____

_____

16 Writing a Paragraph of Information

Write about your neighborhood. Ask a family member to help you.

1. Plan a booklet about neighborhood services near your home. The purpose of the booklet is to provide helpful information for family members. Make a list of things that they might need to know. You could include information about schools, information about plumbers or electricians, and information about the locations and types of restaurants, stores, and service stations.

_____

_____

_____

_____

_____

_____

_____

_____

_____

_____

2. Choose one topic about which to write a paragraph. Gather information from a family member or from newspapers. You may want to visit a place of business and ask questions or take notes.

3. Write a rough draft of your paragraph of information. Include a main idea sentence and important details. Do not worry about spelling, punctuation, and grammer yet.

4. Read your paragraph to a family member. Make changes to improve the writing.

5. Check your writing for errors in spelling, punctuation, and grammar. Circle words you think are misspelled. Find out how to spell them.

6. Make a clean copy of your paragraph. Make sure there are no mistakes. Share your paragraph with family members. You may decide to add more pages to your booklet about neighborhood services. Repeat steps 1–5 each time you want to add information.

17 Nouns

Complete this activity at home.

1. Using an old newspaper or magazine, find an article that interest you.

2. Underline ten nouns in the article.

3. Write the nouns in Column A.

4. In Column B, identify each noun as a person, place, or thing.

5. In Column C, write a more exact noun that could replace each noun in Column A.

A	B	C
_____	_____	_____
_____	_____	_____
_____	_____	_____
_____	_____	_____
_____	_____	_____
_____	_____	_____
_____	_____	_____
_____	_____	_____
_____	_____	_____
_____	_____	_____

6. Read the newspaper or magazine article to a family member. Then read the same article using your more exact nouns. Which nouns are better? Why?

_____

_____

_____

_____

_____

18 | Singular and Plural Nouns

Complete this activity at home.

1. Think of singular nouns about a favorite subject. For example, you might think of nouns about insects or football or stamp collecting.

2. Write each noun. Then write its plural form.

_____

_____

_____

_____

_____

_____

_____

_____

3. Share your list with family members. Ask them to contribute nouns to your list.

_____

_____

_____

_____

_____

_____

_____

_____

4. Make a chart of your nouns. Leave room to add other nouns as you think of them. Add illustrations of your nouns along the sides of the chart. Your chart could be the beginning of a poster to hang on your wall.

19 More Plural Nouns

Play this game at home with a family member.

1. Study the singular and plural forms of the following nouns. The plural forms of the nouns follow special rules.

Singular	Plural
ox	oxen
child	children
foot	feet
goose	geese
man	men
mouse	mice
tooth	teeth
woman	women
deer	deer
elk	elk
moose	moose
trout	trout
salmon	salmon
sheep	sheep

2. Cover the plural forms of the nouns with a sheet of paper.

3. Take turns with a family member giving the plural forms of the nouns. Play tic-tac-toe as you name each correct plural noun. Each time you correctly give the plural form of the noun, write your X or O in the grid. The first player to get three X's or O's in a row wins the game.

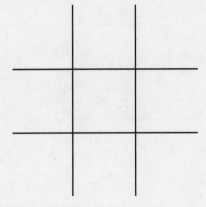

4. Add more nouns to the list, and play the game again.

20 Common and Proper Nouns

Use common and proper nouns to write a paragraph of information about an older family member.

1. Decide which family member you want to write about.

2. Use the following paragraph to help you write about the person. Leave out sentences that do not apply to this person. Add other sentences if you choose. Ask questions to help you find the missing information.

> (Name of person) was born in (city and state) on (day, month, and year). When young, (he or she) attended (name of elementary school). Later, (he or she) attended (name of high school). (He or she) also attended (name of college). On (day, month, and year) (he or she) married (name of person) in (name of place where marriage took place). (He or she) has lived in (towns or cities, states, and perhaps other countries). (Name of person) has worked for (names of companies and where they are located.)

_____

_____

_____

_____

_____

_____

_____

_____

_____

_____

_____

3. Read your paragraph to the family member about whom you wrote. Be sure it is accurate.

4. Make a clean copy of the paragraph to give to the family member.

21 | Names and Titles of People

Write invitations to an art exhibit.

1. Imagine that you are making up a guest list for an art exhibit. You want to invite your friends and your family. You also want to invite famous or well-known people to the exhibit. You hope these people will support the arts in your area.

2. Make a list of people you would invite. You may get names from the telephone book or from a newspaper. You may hear some names on a news program. You may also ask adult family members who they might include. Write your list using complete names and titles. Then rewrite it using abbreviations. For example, you would rewrite Senator John James Jones as Sen. J. J. Jones.

_____

_____

_____

_____

_____

_____

_____

_____

_____

_____

_____

_____

_____

3. Ask an adult family member to look at your list and circle any names and titles that are not written correctly. Try to correct these names and titles yourself.

22 | Capitalization of Proper Nouns

Ask a family member to help you make a family calendar.

1. You will need 12 pieces of blank paper, one for each month of the year.

2. Label one page for each month. Draw lines to divide each month into the correct number of days.

3. Label the days of the week.

4. Number the days of each month.

5. Brainstorm ways to mark and decorate holidays, birthdays, and other special days on your calendar.

_____

_____

_____

_____

_____

_____

_____

_____

_____

6. Mark holidays.

7. Mark family birthdays.

8. Mark birthdays of your friends to remind you to send these friends a birthday card or wish them a happy birthday.

9. Mark any other dates that are important to your family. An example would be an anniversary of some kind. You might also want to add notes about trips or events that your family is planning.

10. Be sure you have capitalized all proper nouns on your calendar.

11. Share your calendar with family members. They may suggest adding more information. You can add information to your calendar as important things happen during the year. Keep your calendar to remind you of this year.

23 | Abbreviations

Play a guessing game using abbreviations.

1. Make a list of words and their abbreviations. You may use words from your textbook and any other words you know, such as the names of states.

_____ _____ _____ _____

_____ _____ _____ _____

_____ _____ _____ _____

_____ _____ _____ _____

_____ _____ _____ _____

_____ _____ _____ _____

2. Ask a family member to add to your list until you have twenty-four pairs of words and their abbreviations.

_____ _____ _____ _____

_____ _____ _____ _____

_____ _____ _____ _____

_____ _____ _____ _____

_____ _____ _____ _____

3. Play a guessing game with a family member. Take turns asking questions about the words and abbreviations. For ideas, look at the examples.

EXAMPLES: What is the abbreviation for the month that comes before February?
(Answer: *Jan.*)
What is the abbreviation for the Latin words that mean "before noon?"
(Answer: A.M.)

24 | Singular Possessive Nouns

Correct a letter for a friend.

1. Imagine that the letter below was written by a friend named Lee. Lee does not understand the difference between plurals and possessives. He sometimes uses awkward wording to avoid using the possessive form. Your friend has asked you to make corrections to his letter. Read the letter carefully. Then rewrite it using the correct possessive forms.

   The mother of Tom asked me to go with their family on a trip to the museum. The days trip was wonderful. One artists work really impressed me. The work of the sculptor was amazing. We toured the museum with a large group of people. The groups interest was mostly in paintings, which hung on every wall. We walked from room to room, our eyes full of wonder. Before we knew it, the museums lights were blinking. We knew then it was time for our visits end. The museums guards checked the rooms to be sure no one was left inside at days end. I wish you had been with us.

   _____

   _____

   _____

   _____

   _____

   _____

   _____

   _____

   _____

   _____

   _____

   _____

   _____

2. Ask a family member to check your work. Discuss the way an apostrophe is used to show a possessive.

25 | Plural Possessive Nouns

Complete this activity at home with a family member.

1. Make up 12 questions about possessive nouns.

   EXAMPLES: If a nest belongs to more than one bird, how do you spell the possessive?
   (Answer: *b i r d s '*)

   If an office belongs to more than one group, how do you spell the possessive?
   (Answer: *g r o u p s '*)

   If an egg belongs to more than one goose, how do you spell the possessive?
   (Answer: *g e e s e ' s*)

   _____
   _____
   _____
   _____
   _____
   _____
   _____
   _____
   _____
   _____
   _____
   _____
   _____
   _____

2. Ask a family member to answer the questions. You may have the person answer aloud or write the answer on a sheet of paper.

26 | How-to Paragraph

Complete this activity at home.

1. Read the directions with a family member.

   To make a peanut butter and banana sandwich, you will need two slices of whole-grain bread, peanut butter, and a small, ripe banana. You will also need a small bowl, a spoon, and a fork. First, peel the banana. Break it into small pieces, and put the pieces in the bowl. Then, use the fork to mash the banana. Next, add a heaping spoonful of peanut butter to the banana. Mix the peanut butter and banana together. Last, put half of the mixture on one slice of bread. Put the other slice of bread on top of the mixture. Do not forget to cover the peanut butter and banana mixture that you did not use and put it in the refrigerator. You can use it to make another sandwich later. Eat your sandwich carefully. The banana makes the peanut butter slippery. Enjoy!

2. Discuss the directions with a family member. Are they clear? Can some things be left out? Do they tell you everything you need to know to make a peanut butter and banana sandwich?

3. What changes would you make that might make the directions clearer?

_____

_____

_____

_____

_____

_____

_____

_____

_____

_____

_____

_____

_____

27 Analyzing a How-to Paragraph

Ask a family member to help you learn the directions for a game.

1. Ask an older family member to tell you about games he or she enjoyed at your age. Choose one of the games to learn how to play. Ask the family member to give you more information about the game.

2. Imagine that you are going to write a paragraph about the game. First, you will need a topic sentence. The topic sentence should name the game. Write the topic sentence on the lines.

   _____

   _____

   _____

3. Your paragraph should list the materials that are needed to play the game. Write the materials on the lines.

   _____

   _____

   _____

   _____

   _____

4. Find out where to play the game. Can it be played inside, or is it an outside game?

   _____

   _____

   _____

   _____

5. Find out how many rules there are to the game. Could you write about all the rules of the game in just one paragraph?

6. Think about all you have found out about the game. Do you have all the information that you would need to write a how-to paragraph about the game? Did you remember to find out how to decide who wins the game?

28 | Visualizing Steps in a Process

Draw a map and give directions for a younger person to follow.

1. Draw a map of your neighborhood.

2. Using a colored pencil or pen, draw a line on the map to show the way to get from your house to another place.

3. Imagine that you are going to tell a younger family member how to use the map to go to the place. Think about what the person must do first. Then think about what he or she must do next. Think about each turn the person must make. Think about ways to tell him or her where to turn.

4. Show the map and tell the directions to an older family member. Ask if the map and your directions are clear and easy to follow. Change anything that is not clear.

29 | Writing for an Audience and a Purpose

Complete this activity at home.

1. Read the following directions with a family member.

    It is easy to make a little bag in which you can keep small things. You will need a handkerchief, some cord, a needle, some thread, and a pair of scissors. The size of the bag will depend on the size of the handkerchief. If you use a man's handkerchief, you will have a larger bag than if you use a woman's handkerchief, which is usually smaller. First, turn down 1/2 inch on one edge of the handkerchief. Sew the edge farthest from the fold to make a hem. This gives you a place to put the cord so that you can close the bag. Then, fold the handkerchief in half. The edge where you put the hem should be at the top. Sew across the bottom and up the unfolded side until you come to the hem. Do not sew the hem. Fasten the thread so that it will not come out, and then cut the thread. Put the cord through the hem. Tie the ends of the cord. Now, you can put small items in the bag and pull the cord to close the bag.

2. Talk about the directions. Are they clear? Could someone who does not know how to sew make a bag from a handkerchief? Can some of the information be taken out? Are there more things you need to know?

3. Make changes in the directions, and write a final draft on the lines.

_____

_____

_____

_____

_____

_____

_____

_____

_____

30 | Writing a How-to Paragraph

Complete this activity at home.

1. Imagine that your family has a new pet. It is a very young baby dinosaur. Your family has asked you to write directions for its care so that the baby dinosaur can be left with a baby-dinosaur sitter. Make a list of the things you need to tell the baby-dinosaur sitter.

_____

_____

_____

_____

_____

_____

_____

_____

_____

_____

_____

_____

_____

2. Write a rough draft of your paragraph about how to care for a baby dinosaur. Write down all your ideas. Do not worry about spelling, punctuation, and grammar yet.

3. Read your how-to paragraph to a family member. Make changes to make the writing better.

4. Check your writing for errors in spelling, punctuation, and grammar. Circle any words you think are misspelled. Find out how to spell them.

5. Make a clean copy of your how-to paragraph. Make sure there are no mistakes. Share your paragraph with family members.

31 | Action Verbs

Complete this activity at home.

1. Read the following paragraph.

   Fencewalker the kitten and Wagtail the puppy <u>were going</u> down the path. Suddenly a red ball <u>was</u> in front of them. The ball <u>went on</u> down the path. Fencewalker and Wagtail <u>went</u> after the ball. Wagtail <u>reached</u> the ball first. Wagtail <u>had</u> the ball in his mouth. Fencewalker <u>pushed</u> the ball. It fell out of Wagtail's mouth and <u>went on</u> down the path.

2. Replace the underlined words with strong action verbs. Write the verbs in the blanks.

   Fencewalker the kitten and Wagtail the puppy _____

   down the path. Suddenly a red ball _____ in front of

   them. The ball _____ down the path. Fencewalker and

   Wagtail _____ after the ball. Wagtail _____

   the ball first. Wagtail _____ the ball in his mouth.

   Fencewalker _____ the ball. It fell out of Wagtail's mouth

   and _____ down the path.

3. Ask a family member to replace the underlined words with strong action verbs.

   Fencewalker the kitten and Wagtail the puppy _____

   down the path. Suddenly a red ball _____ in front of

   them. The ball _____ down the path. Fencewalker and

   Wagtail _____ after the ball. Wagtail _____

   the ball first. Wagtail _____ the ball in his mouth.

   Fencewalker _____ the ball. It fell out of Wagtail's mouth

   and _____ down the path.

4. Talk about the action words each of you chose. Which paragraph makes the clearest picture? Why?

32 | Linking Verbs

Write a paragraph to share with a family member.

1. Think about something silly or interesting that happened today at school.

2. Write a paragraph that explains what happened. The paragraph should have at least four sentences. Use at least three linking verbs.

_____

_____

_____

_____

_____

_____

_____

3. Draw a picture to show what happened.

4. Share your paragraph and picture with a family member.

33 | Main Verbs and Helping Verbs

Complete this activity at home.

1. Imagine that you and a family member are on a spaceship. You are going to another planet for a vacation.

2. Write two sentences about what is happening on the spaceship. Use a main verb and a helping verb in each sentence.

_____

_____

_____

_____

_____

_____

_____

3. Write four sentences about what you plan to do when you reach the vacation planet. Use a main verb and a helping verb in each sentence.

_____

_____

_____

_____

_____

_____

_____

4. Share your sentences with a family member.

34 | Verb Tenses

Complete this activity at home.

1. Imagine that you are visiting the zoo with a family member. Choose an animal that you think is interesting.

2. Write two sentences about the animal. Do not tell what the animal is. Use past-tense verbs in each sentence.

_____

_____

_____

_____

3. Write two more sentences about the animal without telling what it is. Use present-tense verbs in each sentence.

_____

_____

_____

_____

4. Write two sentences that tell what you think might happen to the animal next week. Again, don't tell what the animal is.

_____

_____

_____

_____

5. Read your sentences to a family member. Ask him or her to guess which animal your sentences describe.

35 Spelling Present-Tense Verbs

Complete this activity at home with a family member.

1. Read the following paragraph. Fill in the blanks with present-tense verbs. Ask a family member to do this at the same time on a separate sheet of paper.

    Bustifer is a gray kitten, and Shadow is a spotted puppy. They

    _____ many adventures. The kitten _____

    in the white house on the corner. Shadow _____ for

    Bustifer to come out of the white house. Then the puppy and the kitten

    _____ into the garden. Shadow _____ after

    a yellow butterfly. Bustifer_____ up a flower. Shadow's

    owner finds the wilted flower and _____ the puppy home.

    Shadow is in serious trouble! Bustifer _____ in the sun and

    _____ .

2. Write two sentences that tell what happens to Shadow when he gets home. Use present-tense verbs. Make your sentence funny. Ask a family member to do this at the same time.

    _____

    _____

    _____

    _____

3. Read your paragraph to your family member. Ask the family member to read his or her paragraph to you.

4. Share your sentences with your family member.

5. Ask your family member to share his or her sentence with you. Decide which sentence is funnier. Write it on the line.

    _____

36 | Spelling Past-Tense Verbs

Complete this activity at home.

1. Ask a family member to tell you about something silly that happened when he or she was about your age.

2. Write a paragraph that tells about the experience. Use at least four past-tense verbs.

_____

_____

_____

_____

_____

_____

_____

_____

_____

_____

_____

_____

_____

_____

_____

_____

3. Share the paragraph with the family member who told you about the silly experience.

37 | Friendly Letter

Complete this activity at home.

1. Read the following letter.

August 4, 19—

Dear Jeanne,

    We went to the park. We saw a baseball game. We had fun. We had some things to eat. When the game was over, we went home. We had supper. We went to bed early.

Your friend,

Nancy

2. What could the writer have included to make the letter more interesting? Make notes of things that would improve the letter.

_____

_____

_____

_____

_____

_____

_____

3. Ask a family member to read the letter and make notes about what he or she would include in the letter to improve it.

_____

_____

_____

_____

_____

4. Compare your notes. Discuss your ideas with the family member.

38 | Analyzing a Friendly Letter

Complete this activity at home with a family member.

1. Ask a family member to write a friendly letter to you about an interesting event.

2. Tape or paste the letter in the space below.

3. Read the letter that was written to you. In the margins, identify the heading, greeting, body, closing, and signature.

4. Discuss the parts of a friendly letter with family members.

39 | Connecting Cause and Effect

Complete this activity at home with a family member.

1. Watch a news report on television, or listen to radio news with a family member.

2. Each of you should take notes about the news reports by writing down causes and effects. Sometimes the cause of an event is not reported. You may want to write what you think might have been the cause. Sometimes an event is reported without giving an effect. You may want to write what effect you think an event might cause. Write your notes on the lines. Ask your family members to use a separate sheet of paper.

_____

_____

_____

_____

_____

_____

_____

_____

_____

_____

_____

_____

_____

_____

3. Compare your notes with the family member. Did you both write the same causes and effects? Discuss the differences in your notes.

40 | Including Details That Tell Why

Complete this activity at home.

1. You will need an old magazine that you may cut up.

2. Cut out five pictures from the magazine. Be sure each picture shows some action.

3. Decide what is happening in each picture and why. Think of details that tell why the action is happening.

> **EXAMPLE:** Picture: A young girl is sitting on the bench at the side of the basketball court. A towel is around her shoulders. She is perspiring. Her hands are hanging at her sides. Her head is bent.
>
> Details that tell why: The girl has just made the last foul she is allowed. She is benched for the rest of the game. She is sad because she is a good scorer and her team is losing.

4. Make notes about each picture and the details that tell why the action in the picture is happening.

_____

_____

_____

_____

_____

_____

_____

_____

_____

_____

5. Read the details to a family member. Ask him or her to try to decide which picture the details explain. If he or she has difficulty, try to make your details explain the picture more clearly.

41 Writing a Friendly Letter

Complete the activity at home.

1. Write a friendly letter as though you are a character in a book writing to a character in another book.

2. Make a list of things you would like to write about in a friendly letter. Choose one of these things as the focus of the letter.

_____

_____

_____

_____

3. Write down ideas about the thing you have selected as your focus.

_____

_____

_____

_____

_____

4. Write a draft of your letter. Be sure you write the ideas in a logical order. Do not worry about spelling, punctuation, and grammar yet.

5. Reread your letter. Think about the character who will receive the letter. Will that character be able to understand everything you have said? If not, make changes. Ask a family member to read the letter and make suggestions for improving it.

6. Check your writing for errors in spelling, punctuation, and grammar. Circle any words you think are misspelled. Find out how to spell them.

7. Make a clean copy of your letter. Be sure there are no mistakes. Share the letter with the family member who read your draft.

42 | Agreement of Subjects and Verbs

Complete the activity at home.

1. You will need a page from an old newspaper or magazine and two different colored pencils or pens.

2. Underline each singular verb on the page with a colored pen or pencil. Draw a line around the subject of each verb and a line connecting the subject to the verb.

3. Do the same thing with plural verbs and subjects. Use a different colored pen or pencil.

4. Discuss your markings with a family member.

5. Think about your own use of subjects and verbs. Think especially about the agreement of pronouns and forms of the verb *be*. Ask a family member to help you eliminate agreement errors from your speech and writing.

6. Make a list of the errors you would like to correct.

_____

_____

_____

_____

_____

_____

_____

_____

7. Choose one error that you would like to correct. Write it on the line.

_____

8. Work out a private signal with the family member, such as pulling on an earlobe. When you make an error, the family member can quietly give you the signal. Try to correct the agreement error right away.

43 | Irregular Verbs

Complete this activity at home.

1. Read the following letter. Note that it is written in the present tense.

July 23, 19—

Dear Jon,

This afternoon I go to the lake. I want to have a swim. I have a towel with me, and I am wearing my swimsuit, so I just jump right into that cool water. Pretty soon a pretty flock of geese fly over. They are flying right over my head. I can see that they don't even know I'm down here in their water. They land near me and begin squawking and dipping down into the water for fish. I get so interested in watching these beauties that I almost forget to go home for dinner. When I get home, I just can't get the geese out of my head. I wish you are there to see them.

Best wishes,

Mike

2. Rewrite the letter in the past tense. You may add, delete, and change sentences to improve the letter.

_____

_____

_____

_____

_____

_____

_____

_____

_____

_____

3. Ask a family member to review your letter and discuss it with you.

44 More Irregular Verbs

Complete this activity at home with a family member.

1. Make a list of five irregular verbs. List the present tense form, the past tense form, and the form used with *have, has,* or *had.* Use another sheet of paper if you need more room.

Present	Past	Past with *have, has,* or *had*

2. Use the verbs to write sentences. Ask a family member also to write sentences on a separate sheet of paper.

_____

_____

_____

_____

_____

_____

_____

_____

_____

_____

3. Take turns reading your sentences to each other. The listener must identify the tense that is used in the sentence.

45 Contractions with *Not*

Make and play a game with contractions.

1. Write a list of twelve contractions made with the word *not*. Also, list the words from which they are formed.

_____

_____

_____

_____

_____

_____

_____

_____

_____

_____

2. You will need twenty-four 3″ x 5″ cards or squares of paper. Write the contractions on twelve cards. On the other twelve cards, write the words from which each contraction is formed.

3. Mix up the twenty-four cards, and lay them face down in a grid of six cards by four cards.

4. Play Contraction Mix with a friend.

5. The first player turns over two cards and reads both. The cards are a pair if a contraction is on one card and the words from which the contraction is formed are on the other.

6. If the player has made a pair, he or she keeps it and takes another turn. If the two cards are not a pair, the cards are turned back down in the same place and the other person takes a turn. Continue until all cards have been matched.

7. The person with the most matches at the end of the game is the winner.

46 | Direct Quotations and Dialogue

Complete this activity at home.

1. The story below is written without any dialogue. Rewrite it with as much dialogue as possible. Use another sheet of paper if you need more room.

   A man asked his young son to go to the village with him to sell some eggs. The son said he would. The man said to put the eggs in a basket on the donkey's back and lead the donkey by a rope. The son said he would. After a while, they met a man who said it was foolish for them to walk. He said the boy should ride. The father agreed, and the son got on the donkey's back. Pretty soon they came to another man who said it was cruel of the son to make his father walk. The son agreed and got off. He told his father to climb on. Soon they met a third man. He said it was silly for one to walk and the other to ride when the donkey could easily carry them both. The boy and his father said that made sense. The boy climbed up with his father. The weight was too much for the poor donkey. The donkey fell down and couldn't get up again. All the eggs broke. The father told the boy that it is a mistake to try to take advice from everyone who passes by.

   _____

   _____

   _____

   _____

   _____

   _____

   _____

   _____

   _____

   _____

   _____

   _____

2. Read your story. Be sure you have used quotation marks and other punctuation correctly. Be sure you have used vivid verbs. Share your story with a family member.

47 Fable

Complete the activity at home.

1. Find a fable in a book or magazine. Read the story with a family member. Do not read the moral of the fable.

2. Talk about the characters and events in the story.

3. Write the moral that you learned from the story.

_____

_____

4. Ask your family member to write the moral he or she learned from the story.

_____

_____

5. Compare the morals you wrote. Did you both understand the story in the same way?

6. If you each wrote a different moral, talk about what you wrote. Try to understand why your moral is different from your family member's moral.

7. If both of you wrote the same moral, talk about the things that helped you to understand the meaning of the story. Write them on the lines.

_____

_____

_____

_____

_____

_____

_____

_____

_____

48 | Analyzing a Fable

Complete this activity at home.

1. Read this version of a very old fable.

> As you no doubt know, Turtle moves very slowly. Rabbit runs very fast. Rabbit likes to tease Turtle. One day, Rabbit said to Turtle, "Let's race to the bottom of the hill." Turtle was thinking of something else and agreed. They decided on a starting line and a finish line. Turtle wondered why she had agreed to race.
>
> The animals in the forest gathered at the starting line. The barnyard animals waited at the finish line. Rabbit was sure to win, so everyone cheered for him. Turtle and Rabbit started out together, but Rabbit was soon halfway to the finish line. He decided it would be a good joke to take a nap so that he could say, "I sleep faster than Turtle runs." Rabbit lay down under a tree and went fast asleep. Turtle plodded on steadily.
>
> Turtle was surprised to hear Rabbit snoring as she passed the tree, but she did not stop. After a while, it was Rabbit who was surprised by a sound. All of the barnyard animals were yelling, "Turtle wins! Turtle wins!"

2. On another sheet of paper, make a story map of the fable. Include the characters and setting. Write the beginning, middle, and ending of the fable.

3. The moral is missing. Write a moral for the fable.

_____

_____

_____

_____

_____

_____

_____

_____

4. Share the fable and story map with a family member. Ask him or her whether your moral is a good one.

49 Evaluating Ideas to Support a Conclusion 49

Complete this activity at home with a family member.

1. Think of an object somewhere in your home. Decide what conclusion you want someone to draw about the object. For example, you might think about a chair. The conclusion you want someone to draw is that you like the color of the chair. On the lines, write your conclusion about the object.

_____

_____

2. Write three clues leading to the conclusion you want someone to draw. Do not name the object.

_____

_____

_____

_____

_____

_____

3. Choose the best clue to read to a family member. Ask the family member to try to draw the conclusion you have in mind. If the family member cannot draw the conclusion you have in mind, try to give a better clue. Ask the family member how your clues could have been better.

4. Ask the family member to choose an object and repeat steps 1–3.

_____

_____

_____

_____

_____

_____

50 Storytelling—Dialogue and Characters

Complete this activity at home.

1. Listen to some television programs that you and other family members enjoy. Pay attention to the special ways certain characters talk.

2. Write some phrases and sentences that you hear favorite characters say. Be sure to write who said each phrase or sentence. Do not try to write whole conversations.

_____

_____

_____

_____

_____

_____

_____

_____

_____

3. Share what you wrote with family members. Say the character's words without telling who said them. Ask your family to identify which character is speaking. Discuss how they can tell who is speaking. Discuss which words give clues about how someone feels. Do some characters have certain expressions they use over and over? On the lines, write notes about your discussion.

_____

_____

_____

_____

51 Writing a Fable

Write a fable for a family member.

1. Talk to older family members about fables or stories they heard or read when they were about your age. Make notes about some of the fables.

_____

_____

_____

_____

_____

2. Choose one of the fables or stories to rewrite for a younger family member. Talk to the person who told the fable to you. Be sure you understand the story. Make notes about the fable.

_____

_____

_____

_____

_____

_____

3. Write a rough draft of the fable. Put in all the characters and events. Write the moral. Do not worry about spelling, punctuation, and grammar yet.

4. Read the fable to the person who told it to you. Check that the fable is organized correctly. Take out any words that do not help the story.

5. Check your writing for errors in spelling, punctuation, and grammar. Circle any words you think are misspelled. Find out how to spell them.

6. Make a clean copy of your fable. Make sure there are no mistakes. In the margins, draw pictures of the characters. Share your fable with family members.

52 Pronouns

Complete this activity at home.

1. Write a paragraph about something funny that happened to a person named Captain Dawkins. Begin each sentence with the words *Captain Dawkins*. Write at least three sentences in your paragraph.

_____

_____

_____

_____

_____

_____

_____

2. Write the paragraph again. Except for the first sentence, change the words *Captain Dawkins* to a pronoun.

_____

_____

_____

_____

_____

_____

_____

3. Read both paragraphs to a family member. Discuss which paragraph is better and why.

53 | Subject Pronouns

Complete this activity at home.

1. Imagine that you and your family are traveling into the future in a time machine. In the next century, you are going to visit a circus called Futurecircus.

2. Write five pairs of sentences about Futurecircus. In the first sentence, use a noun as the subject of the sentence. In the second sentence, use a subject pronoun. Make sure the second sentence gives a detail about the first sentence.

_____

_____

_____

_____

_____

_____

_____

_____

_____

_____

3. Share you sentences with a family member. Ask him or her if the second sentence in each pair describes a detail in the first sentence. If it does not, try writing another second sentence. On the lines or on a separate sheet of paper, write your new sentences.

_____

_____

_____

_____

54 | Object Pronouns

Complete this activity at home with a family member.

1. Find an article that interests you in an old newspaper or magazine.

2. Carefully cut out the article and paste or glue it in the space below.

3. Read the article. Draw a box around each object pronoun in the article. When you are finished, ask a family to read the article and draw a box around any object pronouns that you missed.

4. Look at each sentence that has a box in it. In the margin, write a noun that could replace the object pronoun.

Name _____

55 | *I, Me, We, Us*

Complete this activity at home.

1. Imagine that your family owns a baby panda. The editor of a newspaper has asked you to write a story about how the baby panda has changed the lives of everyone in your family. Discuss with a family member how you might feel and what you might do to care for a baby panda. Take notes about what you discuss.

_____

_____

_____

_____

_____

_____

2. Write a paragraph about how you and your family like having a baby panda. Use the subject pronouns *I* and *we* and the object pronouns *me* and *us* at least once in the paragraph.

_____

_____

_____

_____

_____

_____

_____

_____

3. Share your paragraph with family members.

56 | Agreement of Subject Pronouns with Verbs

Play a matching game with a family member.

1. Use 3" x 5" cards or squares of paper to make game cards. Make one card for each of the pronouns *he, she, it, I, you, we,* and *they.* Choose 10 verbs. Write the singular and plural forms of the verbs on the lines. Make one card for the singular form of each verb. Make another card for the plural form of each verb. You will have 20 verb cards.

_____

_____

_____

_____

_____

_____

_____

_____

_____

_____

2. Turn the pronoun cards face down in a stack. Mix up the verb cards, and turn them face down in a separate stack.

3. The first player picks up a pronoun card and a verb card. If the pronoun and verb agree, the player keeps the verb card and returns the pronoun card to the bottom of the stack of pronoun cards. If the pronoun and verb do not agree, the player returns the verb card to the pile of verb cards and places the pronoun card on the bottom of the stack of pronoun cards.

4. The next player repeats step 2. The game continues until all of the verb cards are gone. The player who has the most verb cards at the end of the game is the winner.

57 | Possessive Pronouns

Complete this activity at home with family members.

1. Listen carefully to a conversation that your family members are having. Each time a family member uses a possessive pronoun, place a check mark in that column.

my	your	his	her	its	our	their

2. When the conversation has ended, share the results with your family members. Which possessive pronoun was used most? Which one was used least?

58 | Contractions with Pronouns

Play a contraction construction game with a family member.

1. Use 3" x 5" cards or squares of paper to make game cards. Make one card for each of the pronouns *he, she, it, I, you, we,* and *they.* Make one card for each of the verbs *am, is, are, have, has, had, would,* and *will.* You will have seven pronoun cards and eight verb cards.

2. Put the pronoun cards face down in one stack and the verb cards face down in another stack.

3. The first player takes one card from each stack. The player then tries to make a contraction from the pronoun and the verb. If the player can make a contraction, write the contraction on the score card. Return the pronoun card to the bottom of the stack of pronoun cards. Return the verb card to the bottom of the stack of verb cards.

4. The next player repeats step 3. Continue the game for five minutes. The player who has the most correct contractions on her or his score card at the end of five minutes is the winner.

Score Card	
Player 1	**Player 2**
_____	_____
_____	_____
_____	_____
_____	_____
_____	_____
_____	_____
_____	_____
_____	_____

59 Description

Make a scrapbook of advertisements that appeal to the senses.

1. Look for advertisements in old newspapers and magazines for products that people use in their homes. Cut out and collect advertisements that appeal to one of the senses.

   EXAMPLES: touch—skin lotion, fabric softener
   taste—food, toothpaste
   hearing—stereo system
   sight—home furnishings, clothing
   smell—flowers, room freshener

2. Paste or glue each advertisement to a separate sheet of paper.

3. Under each advertisement, list the vivid words that have been used to appeal to the senses.

4. Arrange the advertisements in a scrapbook. Put all the advertisements together that appeal to one sense.

5. Share your scrapbook with family members. Underline words that are repeated or used in several advertisements.

6. Try to think of other words that would be appealing to each of the senses. Write these words on the lines.

_____

_____

_____

_____

_____

_____

_____

_____

60 | Analyzing a Descriptive Paragraph

Complete this activity at home with a family member.

1. With a family member, read the following paragraphs. Decide which is more appealing to each of you.

> There's something about a circus that really excites me. I think it's the combination of colors. The bright fluorescent shades of the clowns' clothing mean to me that the audience is going to have a wonderful show. Brightly costumed acrobats spin and twirl like colorful tops. Animal trainers dressed in flashy costumes put the trained animals through their stunts. All the colors combine to make a dazzling picture for the eyes.

> Certain sounds mean circus to me. I can cover my eyes and hold my nose, but as soon as I hear that piping calliope music I know there's a circus nearby. All the magical sounds come rushing in—the screeching trumpet of elephants, the yawning roar of lions and tigers, the shrill whinny of horses. Then there's the drum roll. It starts with a whisper and gets louder and louder until the tension is unbearable. You just know someone is walking a tightrope fifty heart-stopping feet in the air.

2. Discuss with your family member which paragraph matched your feelings best and why.

3. Try replacing the describing words with other vivid words. Try to increase the appeal to the senses. On the lines, write the words and their replacements.

_____

_____

_____

_____

_____

_____

_____

_____

_____

_____

HBJ material copyrighted under notice appearing earlier in this work.

61 Observing Details

Complete this activity at home with a family member.

1. Take this paper and a pencil to a window where you can work for a while without anyone seeing you.

2. Look out the window. In the space below, make a cluster diagram of what you see. Begin by naming the entire scene or large objects in your view. Then add details.

3. When you have completed diagramming what you see, show your diagram to a family member. Ask that person to try to identify the window from which you looked.

4. Look out the window with the family member. Ask him or her for other details that might be missing from your diagram.

62 | Using Metaphors and Similes

Play this verbal game with family members.

1. Tell your family that the purpose of the game is to find the best way to describe something by using similes and metaphors.

2. Be ready to explain similes and metaphors. A simile compares things by using *like* or *as*. A metaphor compares things by saying one thing is something else.

   Simile: The moon is *like* a silver dish in the sky.
   Metaphor: The moon *is* a silver dish hanging in the sky.

3. One person begins by choosing an object in the room and making up a simile that helps describe that thing. The next person tries to make up a stronger simile. Write the similes on the lines. When no one can think of any more similes, switch to metaphors. Keep going until you all agree that you have the best simile and the best metaphor for that thing.

_____
_____
_____
_____
_____
_____
_____
_____
_____
_____
_____
_____

4. The next person picks something else and begins with a simile. Continue in the same manner.

63 | Writing a Descriptive Paragraph

Complete this activity at home.

1. Make a list of favorite places in your home. You could list special rooms or certain parts of a room. Choose one place as a topic about which to write.

_____

_____

_____

_____

_____

_____

_____

_____

_____

_____

_____

_____

2. Write a rough-draft descriptive paragraph about your topic. Write so that your reader will feel exactly the same way you do about the place. Do not worry about spelling, punctuation, and grammar yet.

3. Read your paragraph to a family member. Ask him or her to say what feeling the paragraph inspires. Discuss what you might change to improve your paragraph. Reread the paragraph to yourself and consider each word to be sure you have chosen the best word you know to describe details and feelings. Make any changes that are necessary.

4. Check your paragraph for errors in spelling, punctuation, and grammar. Circle words that may be misspelled. Find out how to spell them.

5. Make a clean copy of your paragraph. Share it with other family members.

64 | Adjectives

Complete the activity at home.

1. Make an adjective alphabet book. You will need 26 pages for your book, one for each letter of the alphabet.

2. Label the top of each page with a different letter of the alphabet.

3. Think of adjective-and-noun combinations for each letter of the alphabet.

    EXAMPLES: (A) agile alligator, alien acrobat
    (B) blue bicycle, beautiful ballerina

    You may want to use a dictionary or thesaurus to find interesting adjectives. Write your combinations on the lines.

    _____

    _____

    _____

    _____

    _____

    _____

    _____

    _____

    _____

    _____

    _____

    _____

    _____

    _____

4. When you have combinations that you like, write them on the pages of your adjective alphabet book.

5. Make a cover for your alphabet book. Decorate the cover.

6. Share your alphabet book with other family members. Ask them to suggest more entries.

65 | Articles

With family members, make and play a word game using the articles *a, an,* **and** *the.*

1. You will need twenty-seven 3" x 5" cards or squares of blank paper. Divide the cards into three stacks of nine cards each.

2. Make nine article cards for stack one. Three cards should have the word *a*; three cards should have the word *an*; and three cards should have the word *the*. Mix these cards and place them in a stack.

3. Stack two should have nine singular-noun cards. Three of the nouns should begin with a vowel sound. Write the nouns on the lines below. Then write the nouns on the cards. Mix these cards and place them in a stack.

_____

_____

_____

_____

_____

_____

_____

4. Stack three should have nine direction cards. Three cards should say *Add one adjective, and make a sentence.* Three cards should say *Add two adjectives, and make a sentence.* Three cards should say *Add one or two adjectives, make the noun plural, and make a sentence.* Mix these cards, and place them in a stack.

5. Players take turns drawing one card from each stack and following the directions. For example, the first player might draw the article card *a*, the noun *apple*, and the direction *Add two adjectives, and make a sentence.* The response might be: *Tom had a large, juicy apple for lunch.*

6. The other players decide whether the sentence is acceptable. If not, the player has a second chance.

7. When the player is finished, he or she places the cards in a discard pile. The next player then takes a card from each stack.

8. Continue playing until all of the cards have been used.

66 | Adjectives That Follow Linking Verbs

Complete the activity at home.

1. Make a sentence flip-it book. You will need thirty 3″ x 5″ cards and a three-ring binder.

2. Divide the cards into three groups of 10 cards each.

3. Write a noun and a linking verb on each card in the first group. For example, you might write *The cats are* or *The house was.* Be sure to capitalize the first word on each of these cards.

4. Write an adjective and the word *and* on each card in the second group. For example, you might write *strange and* or *old and.*

5. Write another adjective on each card in the third group. Place a period after each adjective in this group.

6. Punch a hole in the top of each card. Put all the noun and linking verb cards on the first ring. Put the set of adjective cards that include the word *and* on the second ring. Put the adjective cards that end with a period on the third ring. You may also attach the cards by using pieces of string. Put the noun and linking verb cards in the first stack. Put the adjective cards with *and* in the second stack. Put the adjective cards that end with a period in the third stack.

7. Flip the cards on each ring to any combination of cards. Have a family member read the silly sentence that results. Add more index cards as you think of different nouns and adjectives to use. Write your favorite silly sentences on the lines.

_____

_____

_____

_____

_____

_____

_____

_____

67 | Adjectives That Compare: with *er, est*

Make up thought-twisters using adjectives that compare.

1. Read the following thought-twisters.

   Easy: If Tom is taller than Sam and Sam is taller than Joe, who is the tallest one of all? (Answer: *Tom*)

   Harder: If Tom is taller than Sam and Sam is shorter than Joe, who is taller, Sam or Joe? (Answer: *Joe*)

   Hardest: If Tom is taller than Sam and Sam is shorter than Joe, who is tallest one of all? (Answer: *There is no way to know. You know that both Tom and Joe are taller than Sam. However, there is no way to tell whether Tom or Joe is taller than the other.*)

2. Make up your own thought-twisters using adjectives that compare.

   _____

   _____

   _____

   _____

   _____

   _____

   _____

   _____

   _____

   _____

   _____

   _____

3. Try some of your thought-twisters on family members. Tell your listener to pay close attention because some thought-twisters are going to be tricky. Be sure you can explain the correct answer before you try them on other people.

68 | Adjectives That Compare: with *More, Most*

Rewrite a story and share it with a family member.

1. In the following story, the wrong form of comparison has sometimes been used. Sometimes, awkward wording has been used when a comparison word would be better. Read the story. Then rewrite it with the correct comparisons.

> Once upon a time, Goldilocks went for a walk in the woods. It was more scary than any place she had ever been. She came to a house and went in. That house was just right. She saw three bowls of porridge. One bowl was too hot. The second was too cold. The third one was more cold than the first one and more hot than the second one. She ate it quickly. Then Goldilocks was the most sleepy that she had ever been. She went upstairs and found three beds. One was too hard. The second was too soft. The third was comfortabler than any bed in which she had ever slept.

_____

_____

_____

_____

_____

_____

_____

_____

_____

_____

_____

_____

_____

2. Share both versions of the story with a family member. Ask him or her which version is easier to understand and why.

69 Adjectives That Compare: Special Forms

Make and play this game at home.

1. Rule four pieces of cardboard into 25 squares each, five squares by five squares.

2. Make a list of the three forms of twenty adjectives: ten that form comparisons with *er* and *est*; five that form comparisons with the words *more* and *most*; and five that have special forms such as *good, better, best.*

_____

_____

_____

_____

_____

_____

_____

_____

_____

_____

3. In each square of one playing card, write one adjective. Each square should have a different adjective.

4. Prepare the other cards using the same words, but write the words in different squares. No two cards should be alike.

5. Write each adjective on a separate slip of paper. Mix them up before each game. Use the list from step 2 to check the responses of the winner.

6. One person is the caller. The players each have a playing board and enough small pieces of paper to cover 25 squares. The caller reads an adjective, and each player puts a marker on that square. When a player has a straight line, he or she says, "Bingo." The winner must read back each adjective and give the other comparative forms. The winner is the caller for the next game.

70 | Persuasion

Complete this activity at home with a family member.

1. In a newspaper or magazine, find an article that tries to persuade. The article should be about a subject that interests you. If you cannot find an article in a magazine or newspaper, look for a passage in a story in which one character tries to persuade another character.

2. Read the article or passage to yourself.

3. Write the question that the article or passages poses.

    _____

    _____

4. Ask a family member to read the same article or passage.

5. Ask your family member to write the question the article or passage poses to him or her.

    _____

    _____

6. Compare your question to your family member's question. Did you both write the same question?

7. Talk about how the article or passage tries to persuade the reader. Does the article or passage persuade you? Why or why not?

    _____

    _____

    _____

    _____

    _____

    _____

    _____

    _____

8. Take turns reading the part that you found most persuasive.

71 Analyzing a Persuasive Paragraph

Complete this activity at home.

1. Find an advertising article in a magazine or newspaper. Advertising articles look almost like regular articles or stories. They can be identified by the word *Advertisement* printed in small letters in a top or bottom corner.

2. Find the topic sentence. Write it on the lines.

   _____

   _____

   _____

   _____

3. Find three detail sentences that give reasons, facts, or examples. Write the sentences on the lines.

   _____

   _____

   _____

   _____

   _____

   _____

   _____

   _____

4. Find a sentence that tells what action the writer wants the reader to take. Write it on the lines.

   _____

   _____

   _____

5. Share the advertising article with a family member. Show him or her your sentences. Discuss whether the advertisement persuades you to try the product.

72 | Classifying Fact and Opinion

Complete this activity at home with a family member.

1. You will need two sheets of paper and two pencils or pens.

2. Talk with a family member about something that interests both of you.

3. Write sentences about the subject. Write some opinion sentences and some fact sentences. Remember that a fact tells something that can be proved. An opinion cannot be proved because it tells the way someone feels or thinks.

_____

_____

_____

_____

_____

_____

_____

_____

_____

_____

_____

_____

4. Ask your family member to write sentences about the subject on a separate sheet of paper.

5. Read one of your sentences to your family member. Ask him or her to decide whether the sentence is fact or opinion.

6. If you both agree, ask your family member to read a sentence to you. Decide whether the sentence is fact or opinion.

7. If you do not agree as to whether the sentence is fact or opinion, discuss why you do not agree.

8. Take turns reading sentences and deciding whether each one is fact or opinion.

73 | Using Examples

Make and play this game at home with a family member.

1. You will need a newspaper or magazine and 3″ x 5″ cards or squares of paper to make game cards.

2. Find at least five sentences that are general facts. More than five will make the game more fun. Copy each sentence on a separate game card.

3. Write an example to support each general fact.

_____

_____

_____

_____

_____

_____

_____

_____

_____

_____

4. Write each example on a separate game card.

5. You will have 10 game cards—five general facts and five examples. Mix up the game cards. Put them in one stack. Each player draws two cards.

6. If the first player has a general fact sentence and the example that supports that fact, he or she shows them to the other player. If the other player agrees that the cards match, the first player puts the cards aside and takes two more cards from the pile.

7. If a player has two cards that do not match, he or she keeps one card and puts the other card on the bottom of the pile. The player takes a new card from the pile, and play passes to the other player.

8. Play until all the cards are matched. The player who has the most pairs at the end of the game is the winner.

74 | Writing a Persuasive Paragraph

Write a persuasive paragraph with the help of a family member.

1. Think about this sentence.

   _____ would make our world a _____ place.

2. Make a list of pairs of words that could complete the sentence. Circle the pair that you think would make the best topic sentence for a persuasive paragraph.

   _____

   _____

   _____

   _____

   _____

   _____

   _____

   _____

   _____

   _____

   _____

3. Write a rough draft of your persuasive paragraph. Start with the topic sentence. Add some opinions and some facts. Write at least one general fact with a supporting example. Do not worry about spelling, punctuation, and grammar yet.

4. Read your persuasive paragraph to a family member. Make changes to make the paragraph better.

5. Check your paragraph for errors in spelling, punctuation, and grammar. Circle any words you think are misspelled. Find out how to spell them.

6. Make a clean copy of your paragraph. Make sure there are no mistakes. Share your persuasive paragraph with a family member.

75 Adverbs

Complete this activity at home.

1. Imagine that a baby elephant has followed you home from school. Write three sentences that explain how this happened. Each sentence should include an adverb that tells *when* or *where*.

_____

_____

_____

_____

_____

2. Imagine that you really like this baby elephant and want very much to keep it. Write three sentences to persuade your family that the elephant would be a good pet. Each sentence should include an adverb that tells *when* or *where*.

_____

_____

_____

_____

_____

3. Share your sentences with your family. Did you succeed in persuading them to let you keep the elephant? Why or why not?

_____

_____

_____

_____

76 More Adverbs

Complete this activity at home.

1. Think about something you have done that was very difficult for you to do. Maybe it was the first time you went somewhere alone, or maybe it was passing a test for which you had to study very hard.

2. Write five sentences that tell about the difficult activity. In each sentence, use one adverb that tells *how*.

_____

_____

_____

_____

_____

_____

_____

_____

_____

3. Read your sentences to a family member. The first time you read a sentence, leave out the adverb. Then read the sentence again and include the adverb. Ask which sentence is more vivid. Ask your family member to try to think of another adverb that might fit. How does changing or leaving out the adverb change the sentence?

_____

_____

_____

_____

_____

77 | Adverbs That Compare

Complete this activity at home.

1. Read the paragraph. Fill in the blanks with adverbs that compare.

   Kittens are interesting pets. They learn many things _____

   than puppies do. They learn tricks _____ than puppies learn.

   The thing they do _____ of all is curl up in someone's lap. You

   may have to give a puppy a bath, but kittens will keep themselves clean

   _____ . You never know about kittens. Sometimes they can

   behave_____ . Other times they act _____ .

2. Read the paragraph again, but use different adverbs this time.

   Kittens are interesting pets. They learn many things _____

   than puppies do. They learn tricks _____ than puppies learn.

   The thing they do _____ of all is curl up in someone's lap. You

   may have to give a puppy a bath, but kittens will keep themselves clean

   _____ . You never know about kittens. Sometimes they can

   behave_____ . Other times they act _____ .

3. Explain how using different adverbs changes the meaning of the sentences.

   _____

   _____

   _____

   _____

   _____

   _____

   _____

   _____

78 | Negatives

Complete this activity at home.

1. Imagine that you are a castaway. You have been shipwrecked on an island, and you are all alone. One day you find a bottle on the beach. Inside is a blank piece of paper and a pencil.

2. Write a note to put in the bottle. Tell how you feel about being all alone on the island. Write at least five sentences. Use a negative in each sentence.

_____

_____

_____

_____

_____

_____

_____

_____

_____

_____

_____

_____

_____

_____

_____

_____

_____

3. Share your sentences with family members. Ask how they would feel about being all alone on a desert island.

79 | Adverb or Adjective?

Complete this activity at home.

1. Imagine that you have just returned from a trip in a time machine. You have traveled into the future and into the past. The editor of the local newspaper has asked you to write some stories about your adventures.

2. Decide which adventure you would write about first.

3. Write a paragraph that could be a part of your most interesting adventure. Use adverbs and adjectives to make your writing exciting.

_____

_____

_____

_____

_____

_____

_____

_____

_____

_____

4. Use two colored pencils. With one pencil, draw a line under each adjective. With the other colored pencil, draw a line under each adverb.

5. Share your paragraph with your family. Ask for suggestions for other adverbs and adjectives. How does changing the adverbs and adjectives change your paragraph?

_____

_____

_____

_____

80 | Research Report

Do this activity with a family member.

1. Read the following paragraphs from a research report. Think about the questions the writer had in mind: Who is my audience? What is my topic? What are the main points I want to make?

Stop and Go

Would you be surprised to learn that years ago getting automobiles to stop was just as important as getting them to go? Imagine an intersection of two busy streets. Automobiles were going in both directions on both streets. Drivers were confused. Accidents were common. No traffic lights kept the traffic moving smoothly.

Before 1923, only a couple of methods were used to control traffic. Sometimes a stop-and-go sign was placed at a busy intersection. A police officer turned it now and then. Sometimes hand signals were used. Neither of these methods worked very well.

In the early 1920's, a man named Garrett Morgan saw an accident and decided there had to be a way to make driving safer. In 1923, he received a patent for the first three-way traffic signal. You might say that we owe our lives to this man.

2. Discuss the selection with a family member. How would the report be different if it had been written for people who work in traffic control?

_____

_____

_____

3. How would it be written if the purpose were to tell about Garrett Morgan's life rather than about traffic signals?

_____

_____

_____

_____

_____

81 | Analyzing a Research Report

Complete this activity at home with a family member.

1. The beginnings of two research reports are shown below. They are quite different, but they are alike in some ways. Read them to yourself. Ask a family member to read them also.

   In Japan, a fish-eating bird, the cormorant, is trained to catch hundreds of fish in a single night. It takes two years to train a cormorant to do this. The bird's wings are clipped so that it cannot fly away. It has a metal ring around its neck so that it can swallow only very small fish. A harness goes around its body and under its wings. A leash attaches the bird to its trainer. The trainer takes the cormorant out on a boat and lowers it into the water to dive for fish. The cormorant stores the fish in a large neck pouch. When the pouch is full, the bird is pulled aboard and turned upside-down to empty the fish onto the deck.

   River barges drift beneath a starless summer night sky. Fishers call encouraging words above noisy splashes. Suddenly a bird is hauled out of the water by a leash that binds the bird to a man in a boat. The bird is tipped head down. Fish flood the deck. On a good night, one feathered friend may catch hundreds of fish for its master.

2. Discuss these two paragraphs with a family member. How are they different? How are they the same? Which paragraph includes more information?

3. Which paragraph do you find more interesting? Why?

_____

_____

_____

_____

_____

_____

_____

_____

82 Classifying Information into Categories

Complete this activity at home.

1. Choose a topic that interests you. For example, you might choose to write about pelicans.

2. Make a chart with information about your topic.

3. Share your chart with a family member. Ask him or her to suggest other information that could be added to the chart.

_____

_____

_____

_____

_____

_____

_____

_____

_____

_____

83 | Capturing the Reader's Interest

Complete this activity at home with a family member.

1. Imagine that you are going to write research reports about the following household items:

   a. safety pin   **b.** egg beater   **c.** steam iron   **d.** hair dryer

2. Think about the kind of information that would be included in a report about each of the topics. For each report, write an opening sentence that will capture a reader's interest. Ask your family member to write opening sentences on a separate sheet of paper.

   a. _____

   b. _____

   c. _____

   d. _____

3. Imagine that you have finished the reports. Write a closing sentence for each report. Ask your family member to do the same.

   a. _____

   b. _____

   c. _____

   d. _____

4. Share your openings and closings. Discuss how your sentences are alike and how they are different.

5. Write the best opening and closing on the lines.

   _____

   _____

   _____

84 Writing a Research Report

Complete this activity at home with a family member.

1. Make a list of possible topics about your state. For example, you might list a native animal, insect, or bird; state parks; rivers; crops; or industries. Choose one topic for a research report.

_____

_____

_____

_____

_____

_____

_____

_____

2. Think of questions about your topic for which you would need answers. Write your questions on cards. Gather information from maps and resource books in your home, by asking family members, by making telephone calls, or by doing research at the library. Be sure to note the source of each piece of information.

3. Organize your information into an outline. You may find that you have more than you can use and need to narrow your topic.

4. Write a rough draft of your research report. Do not worry about spelling, punctuation, and grammar yet.

5. Share your rough draft with a family member. Make changes to improve the sequence of information. Be sure your opening captures the reader's interest.

6. Check your report for errors in spelling, punctuation, and grammar. Circle any words you think are misspelled. Find out how to spell them.

7. Make a clean copy of your report. Make sure there are no errors. Make a cover for your report, and share the report with family members.

85 | Compound Subjects

Complete this activity at home.

1. You will need an old newspaper or magazine and a light-colored felt marker or colored pencil.

2. Find an article that interests you. Look for sentences that have compound subjects. Underline the sentences.

3. Draw a box around examples of short sentences. Decide whether any of the sentences can be combined into sentences with compound subjects.

4. Analyze the sentences that have not been combined. Decide why a writer might choose to write two short sentences when the sentences could have been combined. Which is stronger writing? Why?

_____

_____

_____

_____

_____

5. Copy four sentences that you think could be combined without losing the meaning. Rewrite them as two sentences with compound subjects.

_____

_____

_____

_____

_____

6. Read your sentences to a family member. Then read the original sentences to your family member. Ask which sentences are easier to understand.

86 | Compound Predicates

Make and play this game with a family member.

1. You will need thirty 3″ x 5″ cards or squares of paper.

2. Divide the cards into three groups of ten cards each.

3. Write a subject on each card in the first stack. Be sure that some subjects are singular and some are plural.

4. On the lines, write a predicate for each card in the second and third stacks. Be sure that each predicate is different. Then write the predicates on the cards.

_____

_____

_____

_____

_____

_____

_____

_____

_____

_____

_____

_____

5. Mix the cards in each stack, and place them face down.

6. The first player takes one card from each stack. Using the words on the cards, the player then makes a sentence that has a compound predicate. The sentences may be silly, but they must use correct grammar.

7. If the player makes a correct sentence, he or she keeps the cards. Otherwise, the cards are placed in a discard pile.

8. The next player continues by repeating steps 6 and 7. Continue playing until all the cards have been used.

9. The player who has the greatest number of cards at the end of the game is the winner.

87 | Compound Sentences

Complete this activity at home with a family member.

1. The story below has been written without any compound sentences, compound subjects, or compound predicates. Read the story. Then combine some sentences. Rewrite these sentences on the lines. Use compound sentences and compound predicates. Try to make the story better. Ask a family member to do the activity on a separate sheet of paper.

     A lion caught a small mouse. The lion said to the mouse, "I have you now. I am going to eat you for supper."

     The mouse begged the lion to let him go. The lion wouldn't. The mouse said, "Let me go. I will tell everyone how kind you are. Maybe I will help you some day."

     The lion thought this was silly. The mouse was too small to make a very good supper. He let the mouse go.

     The next day the lion was caught in a hunter's net. He was roaring. He was crying in pain. The mouse said, "I will help you."

     The lion said the mouse was too small. He said the mouse was too weak.

     The mouse said, "My teeth are small. I am grateful to you for letting me go. I will help." The mouse bit. It chewed. It gnawed through the rope. The lion was free.

     "Thank you," roared the lion.

     The mouse smiled. The mouse said, "You did me a favor. I just paid you back."

_____

_____

_____

_____

_____

_____

2. Compare your rewritten story with your family member's story. Did you combine the same sentences or different ones?

88 | Commas in Sentences

Complete this activity at home.

1. On the lines below, add words to each sentence to make it longer. Combine one sentence with another sentence to make a compound sentence, or add nouns, verbs, or adjectives to make a series. You may need to change the form of some of the words.

   EXAMPLES: The robins are singing.
   The robins, bluejays, and sparrows are swooping, soaring, and singing.

   John wants a wagon.
   Carlos, Rosita, and John want a shiny wagon, a scooter, and a new basketball.

   My house is old.

   _____

   _____

   Dad saw clowns at the circus.

   _____

   _____

   Kangaroos hopped.

   _____

   _____

   _____

   The dog barked.

   _____

   _____

2. Read all of your sentences to a family member. Ask your family member for another noun, verb, or adjective to make a series. Add the word to your sentence. Be sure to follow the rules for using commas in sentences.

89 Avoiding Sentence Fragments and Run-on Sentences

Complete this activity at home.

1. The following paragraph has many sentence fragments and run-on sentences. Commas may be needed in some places. Use editing and proofreading marks to make changes.

> The house creaked and groaned as the wind rose over the plains. And blew across our wheat fields. Dad remembered the story of the locusts years ago they had ruined many of the farmers land. We all gathered to listen to the weather news crackling over the radio. Although we feared the electricity would go out any minute. The news was not good the announcer just kept saying, "Wow! This is some storm!" Over and over again. Well, he was right it was some storm. But it didn't help us know what to do next. Finally we decided we had to take shelter. Down in the safety of the cellar. This storm might be just as bad as the locust storm our family would be safe that was the most important thing. We took blankets flashlights water food books and the family pets and marched down the steps. To shelter.

2. On the lines below, rewrite the story correctly.

_____

_____

_____

_____

_____

_____

_____

_____

_____

90 Comparison and Contrast

Complete this activity at home with a family member.

1. Talk with an older family member about what school was like when he or she was in the fourth grade. In the first column, write notes about what your family member tells you about his or her school experiences. In the second column, write notes about what your school experiences are like.

My Family Member's School Experiences　　　　**My School Experiences**

_____　　_____

_____　　_____

_____　　_____

_____　　_____

_____　　_____

_____　　_____

_____　　_____

_____　　_____

_____　　_____

_____　　_____

_____　　_____

_____　　_____

_____　　_____

_____　　_____

2. Read the notes on both schools with your family member. Talk about how your school experiences are alike and different.

91 Analyzing Paragraphs of Comparison and Contrast

Complete this activity at home.

1. Read the following paragraphs with a family member.

> I started school at the same desk where my father began his education. Like him, I was only five years old when I started first grade. My teacher was Mrs. Taylor. She told me that she taught my father the first three years he went to school. She told me to sit in the first desk in the row by the windows. She said that was my father's desk when he was in first grade. The school had two rooms and two teachers for six grades.
>
> However, I went to the two-room school for only one year. That summer the old building was torn down. When I went back to school in the fall, I went to the new school. The new building was larger and had room for more teachers. It had four rooms and a large auditorium. Mrs. Taylor taught first and second grades in one room. Three new teachers taught third through fifth grades in the other rooms. The principal taught the sixth grade, which met in the auditorium.

2. Talk with your family member about the paragraphs. Pick out a topic sentence in each paragraph. Write them on the lines.

_____

_____

_____

_____

3. Which details tell how the writer's school experiences are like the father's? How are the writer's school experiences different from the father's?

_____

_____

_____

_____

_____

92 | Evaluating for Comparison and Contrast

Complete this activity at home with a family member.

1. Think of two television programs that you like to watch. Think about how the programs are alike and how they are different. Talk about the programs with a family member who also watches them.

2. In the columns below, write notes about the programs. Write the name of one program in the space near the top of the first column. Write the name of the other program in the space near the top of the third column.

Things True of Only   **Things True of Only**

_____   _____

_____   _____

_____   _____

_____   _____

_____   _____

_____   _____

_____   _____

_____   _____

_____   _____

_____   _____

_____   _____

3. Show the list to your family member. Ask if he or she agrees with your list. On the lines below, write things that are true of both programs.

_____

_____

_____

93 | Using Formal and Informal Language

Complete this activity at home.

1. In the first column, write a list of informal words and phrases that you hear people say. Also, list examples of informal language that you find in books, magazines, and newspapers. In the second column, write a formal word or phrase that you could use in place of the informal word or phrase.

Informal Words and Phrases	Formal Words and Phrases
_____	_____
_____	_____
_____	_____
_____	_____
_____	_____
_____	_____
_____	_____
_____	_____
_____	_____
_____	_____
_____	_____
_____	_____
_____	_____

2. Share your list with family members. Ask if they can think of other examples of informal language. Add the examples to your list.

94 Writing Paragraphs of Comparison and Contrast

Complete this activity at home with a family member.

1. Talk with members of your family about what life was like when they were about your age. Try to talk to the oldest member of your family or to someone who grew up in a different country. Choose one person's life to compare and contrast to your own life. Talk to the person again. Get all of the information that you can about what the person's life was like when he or she was your age. Write the information on the lines.

_____

_____

_____

_____

_____

_____

_____

_____

_____

_____

2. Write a rough draft of your paragraphs of comparison and contrast. Tell how your life is like that of the other person and how it is different. Write down all the things you think are important. Do not worry about spelling, punctuation, and grammar yet.

3. Read your paragraphs to the family member about whom you are writing. Ask whether the facts you have written about his or her life are correct. Make changes to make the writing better.

4. Check your paragraphs for errors in spelling, punctuation, and grammar. Circle any words you think are misspelled. Find out how to spell them.

5. Make a clean copy of your paragraphs. Make sure there are no mistakes. Share your paragraphs with family members.

95 | Capitalization and End Punctuation of Sentences

Write a paragraph with the help of your family.

1. Talk with family members about your family's history. Find out about the oldest stories that are known about your family.

2. Write a paragraph telling about the oldest event someone in your family remembers. In your paragraph, use at least one declarative, one imperative, one interrogative, and one exclamatory sentence.

_____

_____

_____

_____

_____

_____

_____

_____

_____

_____

_____

_____

_____

3. Share your paragraph with family members. Write one declarative sentence and one imperative sentence to tell their reaction to your paragraph.

_____

_____

_____

_____

96 | Commas Within Sentences

Complete this activity at home.

1. Imagine that you have entered a comma contest. The first prize is a trip around the world. To enter the contest, you must answer the following questions. Be sure to follow the rules for using commas within sentencs.

2. Write one sentence in which you are addressed by your name.

   _____

   _____

   _____

3. Write two compound sentences about the trip around the world.

   _____

   _____

   _____

   _____

4. Write one sentence that lists three places that you would visit on your trip.

   _____

   _____

   _____

5. Write two sentences that begin with *yes*, *no*, or *well*.

   _____

   _____

   _____

   _____

   _____

6. Share your sentences with family members. Ask where they would visit if they could travel around in the world.

97 Capitalization of Proper Nouns and the Pronoun *I*

Complete this activity at home.

1. Think about a special place you would like to visit. Imagine that you are going there. Write a complete sentence to answer each of the following questions.

2. Who will you ask to go with you?

   _____

   _____

3. What is the name of the city or country you want to visit?

   _____

   _____

4. What day of the week do you plan to leave?

   _____

   _____

5. During which month do you plan to travel?

   _____

   _____

6. What are three things or places that you plan to see while you are traveling? Use at least two proper nouns.

   _____

   _____

   _____

   _____

   _____

98 Abbreviations

Start a list to help you remember special days and addresses.

1. People like to have their special days remembered. Everyone has a birthday.
   Many people like to be remembered on other special days as well. Start a list of
   the special days of your family members. When you write down the date of
   each person's special day, write down her or his mailing address. Then on
   important days, you can send a card or a note to each person. Use abbreviations
   where you can.

Special Days and Addresses

Name	Special Day and Date	Mailing Address

2. Share your list with family members. Ask them to help you add to your list.

99 | Letters

Write a letter to share with your family.

1. Imagine that you are living on another planet with your family. Write a friendly letter to someone your age who still lives on Earth. Tell about your school vacation plans. Follow the rules of capitalization and punctuation.

_____

_____

_____

_____

_____

_____

_____

_____

_____

_____

_____

_____

_____

_____

_____

2. Share your letter with your family. Ask how they would like to live on the planet your letter describes.

100 Envelopes

Complete this activity at home with a family member.

1. Complete the two envelopes shown below.

2. Address one envelope to a newspaper. You can get the address from a telephone book or from a copy of the newspaper.

3. Address the second envelope to a friend or relative who lives in another state. Ask someone in your family to help you find an address.

4. Draw and color a stamp on each envelope.

101 Outlines

Complete this activity at home.

1. Think about the things that happened in school this week. Plan how to tell your family a story about your week. Think of ways to make your story funny or interesting.

2. Write an outline for the story about your week. Include at least two main topics. Remember that each main topic must have at least two subtopics. Be sure to give the outline a title.

_____

_____

_____

_____

_____

_____

_____

_____

_____

_____

_____

_____

_____

_____

_____

_____

3. Share the outline with family members. Be prepared to tell the whole story about your week.

102 Titles

Complete this activity at home with family members.

1. Make a list of the titles of your favorite works. Include books, stories, magazines, newspapers, poems, and songs. In the first column, write the title. Be sure to write each title correctly. In the second column, tell the kind of work the title names. In the third column, tell what you like about the work.

My Favorite Works

Title	Kind of Work	Why I Like It

2. Share your list with family members. Ask them about their favorite works.

103 Direct Quotations and Dialogue

Complete this activity at home with a family member.

1. Write a conversation that could take place between two people talking about homework. Make the conversation as funny as you can. Follow the rules for using quotations marks when you are writing direct quotations.

_____

_____

_____

_____

_____

_____

_____

_____

_____

_____

_____

_____

_____

_____

_____

_____

_____

2. Ask a family member to read the dialogue with you. Each of you should choose to be one of the characters. Read the dialogue as if you were talking to each other. After you have read through the dialogue once or twice, read it again for other family members.